Love, K
and
Universal Responsibility

Tenzin Gyatso
The Fourteenth Dalai Lama

Paljor Publications

©Tenzin Gyatso, the XIV Dalai Lama

Published by :
Paljor Publications
D-39, Jangpura Ext.
New Delhi 110 014
India
First print : 1997, Reprint 1999

ISBN:81-86230-06-8

Cover photo : Private Office of H.H. the Dalai Lama,
Theckchen Choeling, Dharamsala

Printed in India by
Archana Advertising
Jangpura, Bhogal
New Delhi

Contents

Publisher's Note

We are pleased to bring out the reprint of this well known book, which is a compilation of three separately documented messages of H.H. the Dalai Lama of Tibet, i.e. *Human Approach to World Peace, Compassion and Individual, The Global Community and the need for Universal Responsibility.* The apostle of peace and non-violence, Dalai Lama has practised the ideal of non-violence to the extreme.

He preached compassion and need for universal brotherhood. As a manifestation of the Buddha of Compassion, his struggle is not confined to Tibetan cause, it has only served as a means through which to crusade for world peace. On December 10, 1989, the World honoured him with the Nobel Peace Prize. His profound yet simply-stated wisdom has received the accolades from the International Community.

The book reveals his philosophy of life, based on the concept of universal responsibility and reverence for all living beings. We are grateful to the Private Office of H.H. the Dalai Lama for bestowing us the honour to make this work available to all. We sincerely pray that messages of His Holiness would guide the sentient beings a long way in their quest for world peace and peace within themselves.

Tsewang Gyalpo   July 6 1999
President

A HUMAN APPROACH
TO WORLD PEACE

Living in society, we should share the sufferings of our fellow citizens and practise compassion and tolerance not only towards our loved ones but also towards our enemies. This is the test of our moral strength.

Introduction

When we rise in the morning and listen to the radio or read the newspaper, we are confronted with the same sad news: violence, crime, wars, and disasters. I cannot recall a single day without a report of something terrible happening somewhere. Even in these modern times it is clear that one's precious life is not safe. No former generation has had to experience so much bad news as we face today; this constant awareness of fear and tension should make any sensitive and compassionate person question seriously the progress of our modern world.

It is ironic that the more serious problems emanate from the more industrially advanced societies. Science and technology have worked wonders in many fields, but the basic human problems remain. There is unprecedented literacy, yet this universal education does not seem to have fostered goodness, but only mental restlessness and discontent instead. There is no doubt about the increase in our material progress and technology, but somehow this is not sufficient as we have not yet succeeded in bringing about peace and happiness or in overcoming suffering.

We can only conclude that there must be something seriously wrong with our progress and development, and if we do not check it in time there could be disastrous consequences for the future of humanity. I am not at all against science and technology— they have contributed immensely to the overall experience of humankind; to our material comfort and well-being and to our greater understanding of the world we live in. But if we give too much emphasis to science and technology we are in danger of losing touch with those aspects of human knowledge and understanding that aspire towards honesty and altruism.

Science and technology, though capable of creating immeasurable material comfort, cannot replace the age-old spiritual and humanitarian values that have largely shaped world civilization, in all its national forms, as we know it today. No one can deny the unprecedented material benefit of science and technology, but our basic human problems remain; we are still faced with the same, if not more, suffering, fear, and tension. Thus it is only logical to try to strike a balance between material development on the one hand and the development of spiritual, human values on the other. In order to bring about this great adjustment, we need to revive our humanitarian values.

I am sure that many people share my concern about the present worldwide moral crisis and will join in my appeal to all humanitarians and religious practitioners who also share this concern to help make our societies more compassionate, just, and equitable. I do not speak as a Buddhist or even as a Tibetan. Nor do I speak as an expert on international politics (though I unavoidably comment on these matters). Rather, I speak simply as a human being, as an upholder of the humanitarian values that are the bedrock not only of Mahayana Buddhism but of all the great world religions. From this perspective I share with you my personal outlook—that

1) universal humanitarianism is essential to solve global problems;

2) compassion is the pillar of world peace;

3) all world religions are already for world peace in this way, as are all humanitarians of whatever ideology;

4) each individual has a universal responsibility to shape institutions to serve human needs.

Solving human problems through transforming human attitudes

Of the many problems we face today, some are natural calamities and must be accepted and faced with equanimity. Others, however, are of our own making, created by misunderstanding, and can be corrected. One such type arises from the conflict of ideologies, political or religious, when people fight each other for petty ends, losing sight of the basic humanity that binds us all together as a single human family. We must remember that the different religions, ideologies, and political systems of the world are meant for human beings to achieve happiness. We must not lose sight of this fundamental goal and at no time should we place means above ends; the supremacy of humanity over matter and ideology must always be maintained.

By far the greatest single danger facing humankind—in fact, all living beings on our planet—is the threat of nuclear destruction. I need not elaborate on this danger, but I would like to appeal to all the leaders of the nuclear powers who literally hold the future of the world in their hands, to the scientists and technicians who continue to create these awesome weapons of destruction, and to all the people at large who are in a position to influence their leaders: I appeal to them to exercise their sanity and begin to work at dismantling and destroying all nuclear weapons. We know that in the event of a nuclear war there will be no victors because there will be no survivors! Is it not frightening just to contemplate such inhuman and heartless destruction? And, is it not logical that we should remove the cause for our own destruction when we know the cause and have both the time and the means to do so? Often we cannot overcome our problems because we either do not know the cause or, if we understand it, do not have the means to remove it. This is not the case with the nuclear threat.

Whether they belong to more evolved species like humans or to simpler ones such as animals, all beings primarily seek peace, comfort, and security. Life is as dear to the mute animal as it is to any human being; even the simplest insect strives for protection from dangers that threaten its life. Just as each one of us wants to live and does not wish to die, so it is with all other creatures in the universe, though their power to effect this is a different matter.

Broadly speaking there are two types of happiness and suffering, mental and physical, and of the two, I believe that mental suffering and happiness are the more acute. Hence, I stress the training of the mind to endure suffering and attain a more lasting state of happiness. However, I also have a more general and concrete idea of happiness: a combination of inner peace, economic development, and above all, world peace. To achieve such goals I feel it is necessary to develop a sense of universal responsibility, a deep concern for all irrespective of creed, colour, sex, or nationality.

The premise behind this idea of universal responsibility is the simple fact that, in general terms, all others' desires are the same as mine. Every being wants happiness and does not want suffering. If we, as intelligent human beings, do not accept this fact, there will be more and more suffering on this planet. If we adopt a self-centered approach to life and constantly try to use others for our own self-interest, we may gain temporary benefits, but in the long run we will not succeed in achieving even personal happiness, and world peace will be completely out of the question.

In their quest for happiness, humans have used different methods, which all too often have been cruel and repellent. Behaving in ways utterly unbecoming to their status as humans, they inflict suffering upon fellow humans and other living beings for their own selfish gains. In the end, such short-sighted actions bring suffering to oneself as well as to others. To be born a human being is a rare event in itself, and it is wise to use this opportunity as effectively and skillfully as possible. We must have the proper perspective, that of the universal life process, so that the happiness or glory of one person or group is not sought at the expense of others.

All this calls for a new approach to global problems. The world is becoming smaller and smaller— and more and more interdependent— as a result of rapid technological advances and international trade as well as increasing transnational relations. We now depend very much on each other. In ancient times problems were mostly family-size, and they were naturally tackled at the family level, but the situation has changed. Today we are so interdependent, so closely interconnected with each other, that without a sense of universal responsibility, a feeling of universal brotherhood and sisterhood, and an understanding and belief that we really are a part of one big human family, we cannot hope to overcome the dangers to our very existence— let alone bring about peace and happiness.

One nation's problems can no longer be satisfactorily solved by itself alone; too much depends on the interest, attitude, and cooperation of other nations. A universal humanitarian approach to world problems seems the only sound basis for world peace. What does this mean? We begin from the recognition mentioned previously that all beings cherish happiness and do not want suffering. It then becomes both morally wrong and pragmatically unwise to pursue only one's own happiness oblivious to the feelings and aspirations of all others who surround us as members of the same human family. The wiser course is to think of others also when pursuing our own happiness. This will lead to what I call 'wise self-interest', which hopefully will transform itself into 'compromised self-interest', or better still, 'mutual interest'.

Although the increasing interdependence among nations might be expected to generate more sympathetic cooperation, it is difficult to achieve a spirit of genuine cooperation, as long as people remain indifferent to the feelings and happiness of others. When people are motivated mostly by greed and jealousy, it is not possible for them to live in harmony. A spiritual approach may not solve all the political problems that have been caused by the existing self-centered approach, but in the long run it will overcome the very basis of the problems that we face today.

On the other hand, if humankind continues to approach its problems considering only temporary expediency, future generations will have to face tremendous difficulties. The global population is increasing, and our resources are being rapidly depleted. Look at the trees, for example. No one knows exactly what adverse effects massive deforestation will have on the climate, the soil, and global ecology as a whole. We are facing problems because people are concentrating only on their short-term, selfish interests, not thinking of the entire human family. They are not thinking of the earth and the long-term effects on universal life as a whole. If we of the present generation do not think about these now, future generations may not be able to cope with them.

Compassion as the pillar of world peace

According to Buddhist psychology, most of our troubles are due to our passionate desire for and attachment to things that we misapprehend as enduring entities. The pursuit of the objects of our desire and attachment involves the use of aggression and competitiveness as supposedly efficacious instruments. These mental processes easily translate into actions, breeding belligerence as an obvious effect. Such processes have been going on in the human mind since time immemorial but their execution has become more effective under modern conditions. What can we do to control and regulate these 'poisons'— delusion, greed, and aggression? For it is these poisons that are behind almost every trouble in the world.

As one brought up in the Mahayana Buddhist tradition, I feel that love and compassion are the moral fabric of world peace. Let me first define what I mean by compassion. When you have pity or compassion for a very poor person, you are showing sympathy because he or she is poor; your compassion is based on altruistic considerations. On the other hand, love towards your wife, your husband, your children, or a close friend is usually based on attachment. When your attachment changes, your kindness also changes; it may disappear. This is not true love. Real love is not based on attachment, but on altruism. In this case your compassion will remain as a humane response to suffering as long as beings continue to suffer.

This type of compassion is what we must strive to cultivate in ourselves, and we must develop it from a limited amount to the limitless. Undiscriminating, spontaneous, and unlimited compassion for all sentient beings is obviously not the usual love that one has for friends or family, which is alloyed with ignorance, desire, and attachment. The kind of love we should advocate is this wider love that you can have even for someone who has done harm to you: your enemy.

The rationale for compassion is that every one of us wants to avoid suffering and gain happiness. This, in turn, is based on the valid feeling of 'I', which determines the universal desire for happiness. Indeed, all beings are born with similar desires and should have an equal right to fulfil them. If I compare myself with others, who are countless, I feel that others are more important because I am just one person whereas others are many. Further, the Tibetan Buddhist tradition teaches us to view all sentient beings as our dear mothers and to show our gratitude by loving them all. For, according to Buddhist theory, we are born and reborn countless number of times, and it is conceivable that each being has been our parent at one time or another. In this way all beings in the universe share a family relationship.

Whether one believes in religion or not, there is no one who does not appreciate love and compassion. Right from the moment of our birth, we are under the care and kindness of our parents; later in life, when facing the sufferings of disease and old age, we are again dependent on the kindness of others. If at the beginning and end of our lives we depend upon others' kindness, why then in the middle should we not act kindly towards others?

The development of a kind heart (a feeling of closeness for all human beings) does not involve the religiosity we normally associate with conventional religious practice. It is not only for people who believe in religion, but is for everyone regardless of race, religion, or political affiliation. It is for anyone who considers himself or herself, above all, a member of the human family and who sees things from this larger and longer perspective. This is a powerful feeling that we should develop and apply; instead, we often neglect it, particularly in our prime years when we experience a false sense of security.

When we take into account a longer perspective, the fact that all wish to gain happiness and avoid suffering, and keep in mind our relative unimportance in relation to countless others, we can conclude that it is worthwhile to share our possessions with others. When you train in this sort of outlook, a true sense of compassion— a true sense of love and respect for others— becomes possible. Individual happiness ceases to be a conscious self-seeking effort; it becomes an automatic and far superior by-product of the whole process of loving and serving others.

Another result of spiritual development, most useful in day-to-day life, is that it gives a calmness and presence of mind. Our lives are in a constant flux, bringing many difficulties. When faced with a calm and clear mind, problems can be successfully resolved. When, instead, we lose control over our minds through hatred, selfishness, jealousy, and anger, we lose our sense of judgement. Our minds are blinded and at those wild moments anything can happen, including war. Thus, the practice of compassion and wisdom is useful to all, especially to those responsible for running national affairs, in whose hands lie the power and opportunity to create the structure of world peace.

World religions for world peace

The principles discussed so far are in accordance with the ethical teachings of all world religions. I maintain that every major religion of the world— Buddhism, Christianity, Confucianism, Hinduism,

Islam, Jainism, Judaism, Sikhism, Taoism, Zoroastrianism— has similar ideals of love, the same goal of benefiting humanity through spiritual practice, and the same effect of making their followers into better human beings. All religions teach moral percepts for perfecting the functions of mind, body, and speech. All teach us not to lie or steal or take others' lives, and so on. The common goal of all moral precepts laid down by the great teachers of humanity is unselfishness. The great teachers wanted to lead their followers away from the paths of negative deeds caused by ignorance and to introduce them to paths of goodness.

All religions agree upon the necessity to control the undisciplined mind that harbours selfishness and other roots of trouble, and each teaches a path leading to a spiritual state that is peaceful, disciplined, ethical, and wise. It is in this sense that I believe all religions have essentially the same message. Differences of dogma may be ascribed to differences of time and circumstance as well as cultural influences; indeed, there is no end to scholastic argument when we consider the purely metaphysical side of religion. However, it is much more beneficial to try to implement in daily life the shared precepts for goodness taught by all religions rather than to argue about minor differences in approach.

There are many different religions to bring comfort and happiness to humanity in much the same way as there are particular treatments for different diseases. For, all religions endeavour in their own way to help living beings avoid misery and gain happiness. And, although we can find causes for preferring certain interpretations of religious truths, there is much greater cause for unity, stemming from the human heart. Each religion works in its own way to lessen human suffering and contribute to world civilization. Conversion is not the point. For instance, I do not think of converting others to Buddhism or merely furthering the Buddhist cause. Rather, I try to think of how I as a Buddhist humanitarian can contribute to human happiness.

While pointing out the fundamental similarities between world religions, I do not advocate one particular religion at the expense of all others, nor do I seek a new 'world religion'. All the different religions of the world are needed to enrich human experience and world civilization. Our human minds, being of different calibre and disposition, need different approaches to peace and happiness. It is just like food. Certain people find Christianity more appealing, others prefer Buddhism because there is no creator in it and everything depends upon your own actions. We can make similar arguments for other religions as well. Thus, the point is clear: humanity needs all the world's religions to suit the ways of life, diverse spiritual needs, and inherited national traditions of individual human beings.

It is from this perspective that I welcome efforts being made in various parts of the world for better understanding among religions. The need for this is particularly urgent now. If all religions make the betterment of humanity their main concern, then they can easily work together in harmony for world peace. Interfaith understanding will bring about the unity necessary for all religions to work together. However, although this is indeed an important step, we must remember that there are no quick or easy solutions. We cannot hide the doctrinal differences that exist among various faiths, nor can we hope to replace the existing religions by a new universal belief. Each religion has its own distinctive contributions to make, and each in its own way is suitable to a particular group of people as they understand life. The world needs them all.

There are two primary tasks facing religious practitioners who are concerned with world peace. First, we must promote better interfaith understanding so as to create a workable degree of unity among all religions. This may be achieved in part by respecting each other's beliefs and by emphasizing our common concern for human well-being. Second, we must bring about a viable consensus on basic spiritual values that touch every human heart and enhance general human happiness. This means we must emphasize the common denominator of all world religions—humanitarian ideals. These two steps will enable us to act both individually and together to create the necessary spiritual conditions for world peace.

We practitioners of different faiths can work

together for world peace when we view different religions as essentially instruments to develop a good heart— love and respect for others, a true sense of community. The most important thing is to look at the purpose of religion and not at the details of theology or metaphysics, which can lead to mere intellectualism. I believe that all the major religions of the world can contribute to world peace and work together for the benefit of humanity if we put aside subtle metaphysical differences, which are really the internal business of each religion.

Despite the progressive secularization brought about by worldwide modernization and despite systematic attempts in some parts of the world to destroy spiritual values, the vast majority of humanity continues to believe in one religion or another. The undying faith in religion, evident even under irreligious political systems, clearly demonstrates the potency of religion as such. This spiritual energy and power can be purposefully used to bring about the spiritual conditions necessary for world peace. Religious leaders and humanitarians all over the world have a special role to play in this respect.

Whether we will be able to achieve world peace or not, we have no choice but to work towards that goal. If our minds are dominated by anger, we will lose the best part of human intelligence— wisdom, the ability to decide between right and wrong. Anger is one of the most serious problems facing the world today.

Individual power to shape institutions

Anger plays no small role in current conflicts such as those in the Middle East, Southeast Asia, the North-South problem, and so forth. These conflicts arise from a failure to understand one another's humanness. The answer is not the development and use of greater military force, nor an arms race. Nor is it purely political or purely technological. Basically it is spiritual, in the sense that what is required is a sensitive understanding of our common human situation. Hatred and fighting cannot bring happiness to anyone, even to the winners of battles. Violence always produces misery and thus is essentially counter-productive. It is, therefore, time for world leaders to learn to transcend the differences of race, culture, and ideology and to regard one another through eyes that see the common human situation. To do so would benefit individuals, communities, nations, and the world at large.

The greater part of present world tension seems to stem from the 'Eastern Bloc' versus 'Western Bloc' conflict that has been going on since World War II. These two blocs tend to describe and view each other in a totally unfavourable light. This continuing, unreasonable struggle is due to a lack of mutual affection and respect for each other as fellow human beings. Those of the Eastern Bloc should reduce their hatred towards the Western Bloc because the Western bloc is also made up of human beings— men, women, and children. Similarly those of the Western bloc should reduce their hatred towards the Eastern bloc because the Eastern bloc is also human beings. In such a reduction of mutual hatred, the leaders of both blocs have a powerful role to play. But first and foremost, leaders must realize their own and others' humanness. Without this basic realization, very little effective reduction of organized hatred can be achieved.

If, for example, the leader of the United States of America and the leader of the Union of Soviet Socialist Republics suddenly met each other in the middle of a desolate island, I am sure they would respond to each other spontaneously as fellow human beings. But a wall of mutual suspicion and misunderstanding separates them the moment they are identified as the 'President of the USA' and the 'Secretary-General of the USSR'. More human contact in the form of informal extended meetings, without any agenda, would improve their mutual understanding; they would learn to relate to each other as human beings and could then try to tackle international problems based on this understanding. No two parties, especially those with a history of antagonism, can negotiate fruitfully in an atmosphere of mutual suspicion and hatred.

I suggest that world leaders meet about once a year in a beautiful place without any business, just to get to know each other as human beings. Then, later, they could meet to discuss mutual and global problems. I am sure many others share my wish that world leaders meet at the conference table in such an atmosphere of mutual respect and understanding of each other's humanness.

To improve person-to-person contact in the world at large, I would like to see greater encouragement of international tourism. Also, mass media, particularly in democratic societies, can make a considerable contribution to world peace by giving greater coverage to human interest items that reflect the ultimate oneness of humanity. With the rise of a few big powers in the international arena, the humanitarian role of international organisations is being bypassed and neglected. I hope that this will be corrected and that all international organizations, especially the United Nations, will be more active and effective ensuring maximum benefit to humanity and promoting international understanding. It will indeed be tragic if the few powerful members continue to misuse world bodies like the UN for their one-sided interests. The UN must become the instrument of world peace. This world body must be respected by all, for the UN is the only source of hope for small oppressed nations and hence for the planet as a whole.

As all nations are economically dependent upon one another more than ever before, human understanding must go beyond national boundaries and embrace the international community at large. Indeed, unless we can create an atmosphere of genuine cooperation, gained not by threatened or actual use of force but by heartfelt understanding, world problems will only increase. If people in poorer countries are denied the happiness they desire and deserve, they will naturally be dissatisfied and pose problems for the rich. If unwanted social, political, and cultural forms continue to be imposed upon unwilling people, the attainment of world peace is doubtful. However, if we satisfy people at a heart-to-heart level, peace will surely come.

Within each nation, the individual ought to be given the right to happiness, and among nations, there must be equal concern for the welfare of even the smallest nations. I am not suggesting that one system is better than another and all should adopt it. On the contrary, a variety of political systems and ideologies is desirable and accords with the variety of dispositions within the human community. This variety enhances the ceaseless human quest for happiness. Thus each community should be free to evolve its own political and socio-economic system, based on the principle of self-determination.

The achievement of justice, harmony, and peace depends on many factors. We should think about them in terms of human benefit in the long run rather than the short term. I realize the enormity of the task before us, but I see no other alternative than the one I am proposing— which is based on our common humanity. Nations have no choice but to be concerned about the welfare of others, not so much because of their belief in humanity, but because it is in the mutual and long-term interest of all concerned. An appreciation of this new reality is indicated by the emergence of regional or continental economic organizations such as the European Economic Community, the Association of South East Asian Nations, and so forth. I hope more such trans-national organizations will be formed, particularly in regions where economic development and regional stability seem in short supply.

Under present conditions, there is definitely a growing need for human understanding and a sense of universal responsibility. In order to achieve such ideas, we must generate a good and kind heart, for without this, we can achieve neither universal happiness nor lasting world peace. We cannot create peace on paper. While advocating universal responsibility and universal brotherhood and sisterhood, the fact is that humanity is organized in separate entities in the form of national societies. Thus, in a realistic sense, I feel it is these societies that must act as the building-blocks for world peace.

Attempts have been made in the past to create societies more just and equal. Institutions have been established with noble charters to combat anti-social forces. Unfortunately, such ideas have been cheated by selfishness. More than ever before, we witness today how ethics and noble principles are obscured by the shadow of self-interest, particularly in the political sphere. There is a school of thought that warns us to refrain from politics altogether, as politics has become synonymous with amorality. Politics devoid of ethics does not further human welfare, and life without morality reduces humans to the level of beasts. However, politics is not axiomatically 'dirty'. Rather, the instruments of our political culture have distorted the high ideals and noble concepts meant to further human welfare. Naturally, spiritual people express their concern about religious leaders 'messing' with politics, since they fear the contamination of religion by dirty politics.

I question the popular assumption that religion and ethics have no place in politics and that religious persons should seclude themselves as hermits. Such a view of religion is too one-sided; it lacks a proper perspective on the individual's relation to society and the role of religion in our lives. Ethics is as crucial to a politician as it is to a religious practitioner. Dangerous consequences will follow when politicians and rulers forget moral principles. Whether we believe in God or karma, ethics is the foundation of every religion.

Such human qualities as morality, compassion, decency, wisdom, and so forth have been the foundations of all civilizations. These qualities must be cultivated and sustained through systematic moral education in a conducive social environment so that a more humane world may emerge. The qualities required to create such a world must be inculcated right from the beginning, from childhood. We cannot wait for the next generation to make this change; the present generation must attempt a renewal of basic human values. If there is any hope, it is in the future generations, but not unless we institute major change on a worldwide scale in our present educational system. We need a revolution in our commitment to and practice of universal humanitarian values.

It is not enough to make noisy calls to halt moral degeneration; we must do something about it. Since present-day governments do not shoulder such 'religious' responsibilities, humanitarian and religious leaders must strengthen the existing civic, social, cultural, educational, and religious organizations to revive human and spiritual values. Where necessary, we must create new organizations to achieve these goals. Only in so doing can we hope to create a more stable basis for world peace.

Living in society, we should share the sufferings of our fellow citizens and practise compassion and tolerance not only towards our loved ones but also towards our enemies. This is the test of our moral strength. We must set an example by our own practice, for we cannot hope to convince others of the value of religion by mere words. We must live up to the same high standards of integrity and sacrifice that we ask of others. The ultimate purpose of all religions is to serve and benefit humanity. This is why it is so important that religion always be used to effect the happiness and peace of all beings and not merely to convert others.

Still, in religion there are no national boundaries. A religion can and should be used by any people or person who finds it beneficial.

What is important for each seeker is to choose a religion that is most suitable to himself or herself. But, the embracing of a particular religion does not mean the rejection of another religion or one's own community. In fact, it is important that those who embrace a religion should not cut themselves off from their own society; they should continue to live within their own community and in harmony with its members. By escaping from your own community, you cannot benefit others, whereas benefiting others is actually the basic aim of religion.

In this regard there are two things important to keep in mind: self-examination and self-correction. We should constantly check our attitude towards others, examining ourselves carefully, and we should correct ourselves immediately when we find we are in the wrong.

Finally, a few words about material progress. I have heard a great deal of complaint against material progress from Westerners, and yet, paradoxically, it has been the very pride of the Western world. I see nothing wrong with material progress per se, provided people are always given precedence. It is my firm belief that in order to solve human problems in all their dimensions, we must combine and harmonize economic development with spiritual growth.

However, we must know its limitations. Although materialistic knowledge in the form of science and technology has contributed enormously to human welfare, it is not capable of creating lasting happiness. In America, for example, where technological development is perhaps more advanced than in any other country, there is still a great deal of mental suffering. This is because materialistic knowledge can only provide a type of happiness that is dependent upon physical conditions. It cannot provide happiness that springs from inner development independent of external factors.

For renewal of human values and attainment of lasting happiness, we need to look to the common humanitarian heritage of all nations the world over. May this essay serve as an urgent reminder lest we forget the human values that unite us all as a single family on this planet.

I have written the above lines
to tell my constant feeling.
Whenever I meet even a 'foreigner'
I have always the same feeling:
'I am meeting another member of the human family.'
This attitude has deepened
my affection and respect for all beings.
May this natural wish be
my small contribution to world peace.
I pray for a more friendly,
more caring, and more understanding,
human family on this planet.
To all who dislike suffering,
who cherish lasting happiness—
this is my heartfelt appeal.

Compassion and
the Individual

The more we care for the happiness of others, the greater our own sense of well-being becomes. Cultivating a close, warmhearted feeling for others automatically puts the mind at ease. This helps remove whatever fears or insecurities we may have and gives us the strength to cope with any obstacles we encounter. It is the ultimate source of success in life.

The purpose of life

One great question underlies our experience, whether we think about it consciously or not: What is the purpose of life? I have considered this question and would like to share my thoughts in the hope that they may be of direct, practical benefit to those who read them.

I believe that the purpose of life is to be happy. From the moment of birth, every human being wants happiness and does not want suffering. Neither social conditioning nor education nor ideology affect this. From the very core of our being, we simply desire contentment. I don't know whether the universe, with its countless galaxies, stars and planets, has a deeper meaning or not, but at the very least, it is clear that we humans who live on this earth face the task of making a happy life for ourselves. Therefore, it is important to discover what will bring about the greatest degree of happiness.

How to achieve happiness

For a start, it is possible to divide every kind of happiness and suffering into two main categories: mental and physical. Of the two, it is the mind that exerts the greatest influence on most of us. Unless we are either gravely ill or deprived of basic necessities, our physical condition plays a secondary role in life. If the body is content, we virtually ignore it. The mind, however, registers every event, no matter how small. Hence we should devote our most serious efforts to bringing about mental peace.

From my own limited experience I have found that the greatest degree of inner tranquillity comes from the development of love and compassion.

The more we care for the happiness of others, the greater our own sense of well-being becomes. Cultivating a close, warmhearted feeling for others automatically puts the mind at ease. This helps remove whatever fears or in securities we may have and gives us the strength to cope with any obstacles we encounter. It is the ultimate source of success in life.

As long as we live in this world we are bound to encounter problems. If, at such times, we lose hope and become discouraged, we diminish our ability to face difficulties. If, on the other hand, we remember that it is not just ourselves but every one who has to undergo suffering, this more realistic perspective will increase our determination and capacity to overcome troubles. Indeed, with this attitude, each new obstacle can be seen as yet another valuable opportunity to improve our mind!

Thus we can strive gradually to become more compassionate, that is we can develop both genuine sympathy for others' suffering and the will to help remove their pain. As a result, our own serenity and inner strength will increase.

Our need for love

Ultimately, the reason why love and compassion bring greatest happiness is simply that our nature cherishes them above all else. The need for love lies at the very foundation of human existence. It results from the profound interdependence we all share with one another. However capable and skilful an individual may be, left alone, he or she will not survive. However vigorous and independent one may feel during the most prosperous periods of life, when one is sick or very young or very old, one must depend on the support of others.

Interdependence, of course, is a fundamental law of nature. Not only higher forms of life but also many of the smallest insects are social beings who, without any religion, law or education, survive by mutual cooperation based on an innate recognition of their inter-connectedness. The most subtle level of material phenomena is also governed by interdependence. All phenomena, from the planet we inhabit to the oceans, clouds, forests and flowers that surround us, arise in dependence upon subtle patterns of energy. Without their proper interaction, they dissolve and decay.

It is because our own human existence is so dependent on the help of others that our need for love lies at the very foundation of our existence. Therefore we need a genuine sense of responsibility and a sincere concern for the welfare of others.

We have to consider what we human beings really are. We are not like machine-made objects. If we were merely mechanical entities, then machines themselves could alleviate all of our sufferings and fulfil our needs. However, since we are not solely material creatures, it is a mistake to place all our hopes for happiness on external development alone. Instead, we should consider our origins and nature to discover what we require.

Leaving aside the complex question of the creation and evolution of our universe, we can at least agree that each of us is the product of our own parents. In general, our conception took place not just in the context of sexual desire but from our parents' decision to have a child. Such decisions are founded on responsibility and altruism— the parents' compassionate commitment to care for their child until it is able to take care of itself. Thus, from the very moment of our conception, our parents' love is directly involved in our creation.

Moreover, we are completely dependent upon our mother's care from the earliest stages of our growth. According to some scientists, a pregnant woman's mental state, be it calm or agitated, has a direct physical effect on her unborn child.

The expression of love is also very important at the time of birth. Since the very first thing we do is suck milk from our mother's breast, we naturally feel close to her, and she must feel love for us in order to feed us properly; if she feels anger or resentment her milk may not flow freely.

Then there is the critical period of brain development from the time of birth up to at least the age of three or four, during which time loving physical contact is the single most important factor for the normal growth of the child. If the child is not held, hugged, cuddled or loved, its development will be impaired and its brain will not mature properly.

Since a child cannot survive without the care of others, love is its most important nourishment. The happiness of childhood, the allaying of the child's many fears and the healthy development of its self-confidence all depend directly upon love.

Nowadays, many children grow up in unhappy homes. If they do not receive proper affection, in later life they will rarely love their parents and, not infrequently, will find it hard to love others. This is very sad.

As children grow older and enter school, their need for support must be met by their teachers. If a teacher not only imparts academic education but also assumes responsibility for preparing students for life, his or her pupils will feel trust and respect and what has been taught will leave an indelible impression on their minds. On the other hand, subjects taught by a teacher who does not show true concern for his or her students' overall well-being will be regarded as temporary and not retained for long.

Similarly, if one is sick and being treated in hospital by a doctor who evince a warm human feeling, one feels at ease and the doctor's desire to give the best possible care is itself curative, irrespective of the degree of his or her technical skill. On the other hand, if one's doctor lacks human feeling and displays an unfriendly expression, impatience or casual disregard, one will feel anxious, even if he or she is the most highly qualified doctor and the disease has been correctly diagnosed and the right medication prescribed. Inevitably, patients' feelings make a difference to the quality and completeness of their recovery.

Even when we engage in ordinary conversation in everyday life, if someone speaks with human feeling we enjoy listening, and respond accordingly; the whole conversation becomes interesting, however unimportant the topic may be. On the other hand, if a person speaks coldly or harshly, we feel uneasy and wish for a quick end to the interaction. From the least to the most important event, the affection and respect of others are vital for our happiness.

Recently I met a group of scientists in America who said that the rate of mental illness in their country was quite high— around twelve percent of the population. It became clear during our discussion that the main cause of depression was not a lack of material necessities but a deprivation of the affection of others.

So, as you can see from everything I have

written so far, one thing seems clear to me: whether or not we are consciously aware of it, from the day we are born, the need for human affection is in our very blood. Even if the affection comes from an animal or someone we would normally consider an enemy, both children and adults will naturally gravitate towards it.

I believe that no one is born free from the need for love. And this demonstrates that, although some modern schools of thought seek to do so, human beings cannot be defined as solely physical. No material object, however beautiful or valuable, can make us feel loved, because our deeper identity and true character lie in the subjective nature of the mind.

Developing compassion

Some of my friends have told me that, while love and compassion are marvelous and good, they are not really very relevant. Our world, they say, is not a place where such beliefs have much influence or power. They claim that anger and hatred are so much a part of human nature that humanity will always be dominated by them. I do not agree.

We humans have existed in our present form for about a hundred thousand years. I believe that if during this time the human mind had been primarily controlled by anger and hatred, our overall population would have decreased. But today, despite all our wars, we find that the human population is greater than ever. This clearly indicates to me that love and compassion predominate in the world. And this is why unpleasant events are "news"; compassionate activities are so much a part of daily life that they are taken for granted and, therefore, largely ignored.

So far I have been discussing mainly the mental benefits of compassion, but it contributes to good physical health as well. According to my personal experience, mental stability and physical well-being are directly related. Without question, anger and agitation make us more susceptible to illness. On the other hand, if the mind is tranquil and occupied with positive thoughts, the body will not easily fall prey to disease.

But of course it is also true that we all have an innate self-centeredness that inhibits our love for others. So, since we desire the true happiness that is brought about only by a calm mind, and since such peace of mind is brought about only by a compassionate attitude, how can we develop this? Obviously, it is not enough for us simply to think about how nice compassion is! We need to make a concerted effort to develop it; we must use all the events of our daily life to transform our thoughts and behaviour.

First of all, we must be clear about what we mean by compassion. Many forms of compassionate feeling are mixed with desire and attachment. For instance, the love parents feel for their child is often strongly associated with their own emotional needs, so it is not fully compassionate. Again, in marriage, the love between husband and wife— particularly at the beginning, when each partner still may not know the other's deeper character very well— depends more on attachment than genuine love. Our desire can be so strong that the person to whom we are attached appears to be good, when in fact he or she is very negative. In addition, we have a tendency to exaggerate small positive qualities. Thus when one partner's attitude changes, the other partner is often disappointed and his or her attitude changes too. This is an indication that love has been motivated more by personal need than by genuine care for the other individual.

True compassion is not just an emotional response but a firm commitment founded on reason. Therefore, a truly compassionate attitude towards others does not change even if they behave negatively.

Of course, developing this kind of compassion is not at all easy! As a start, let us consider the following facts:

Whether people are beautiful and friendly or unattractive and disruptive, ultimately they are human beings, just like oneself. Like oneself, they want happiness and do not want suffering. Furthermore, their right to overcome suffering and be happy is equal to one's own. Now, when you recognize that all beings are equal in both their desire for happiness and their right to obtain it, you automatically feel empathy and closeness for them. Through accustoming your mind to this sense of universal altruism, you develop a feeling of responsibility for others: the wish to help them actively overcome their problems. Nor is this wish selective; it applies equally to all. As long as they are human beings experiencing pleasure and pain just as you do, there is no logical basis to discriminate between them or to alter your concern for them if they behave negatively.

Let me emphasize that it is within our power, given patience and time, to develop this kind of compassion. Of course, our self-centeredness, our distinctive attachment to the feeling of an independent, self-existent "I", works fundamentally to inhibit our compassion. Indeed, true compassion can be experienced only when this type of self-grasping is eliminated. But this does not mean that we cannot start and make progress now.

How we can start

We should begin by removing the greatest hindrances to compassion: anger and hatred. As we all know, these are extremely powerful emotions and they can overwhelm our entire mind. Nevertheless, they can be controlled. If, however, they are not, these negative emotions will plague us— with no extra effort on their part!— and impede our quest for the happiness of a loving mind.

So as a start, it is useful to investigate whether

or not anger is of value. Sometimes, when we are discouraged by a difficult situation, anger does seem helpful, appearing to bring with it more energy, confidence and determination.

Here, though, we must examine our mental state carefully. While it is true that anger brings extra energy, if we explore the nature of this energy, we discover that it is blind: we cannot be sure whether its result will be positive or negative. This is because anger eclipses the best part of our brain: its rationality. So the energy of anger is almost always unreliable. It can cause an immense amount of destructive, unfortunate behavior. Moreover, if anger increases to the extreme, one becomes like a mad person, acting in ways that are as damaging to oneself as they are to others.

It is possible, however, to develop an equally forceful but far more controlled energy with which to handle difficult situations.

This controlled energy comes not only from a compassionate attitude, but also from reason and patience. These are the most powerful antidotes to anger. Unfortunately, many people misjudge these qualities as signs of weakness. I believe the opposite to be true: that they are the true signs of inner strength. Compassion is by nature gentle, peaceful and soft, but it is also very powerful. It is those who easily lose their patience who are insecure and unstable. Thus, to me, the arousal of anger is a direct sign of weakness.

So, when a problem first arises, try to remain humble and maintain a sincere attitude and be concerned that the outcome is fair. Of course, others may try to take advantage of you, and if your remaining detached only encourages unjust aggression, adopt a strong stand. This, however, should be done with compassion, and if it is necessary to express your views and take strong countermeasures, do so without anger or ill-intent.

You should realize that even though your opponents appear to be harming you, in the end, their destructive activity will damage only themselves. In order to check your own selfish impulse to retaliate, you should recall your desire to practice compassion and assume responsibility for helping prevent the other person from suffering the consequences of his or her acts.

Thus, because the measures you employ have been calmly chosen, they will be more effective, more accurate and more forceful. Retaliation based on the blind energy of anger seldom hits the target.

Friends and enemies

I must emphasize again that merely thinking that compassion and reason and patience are good will not be enough to develop them. We must wait for difficulties to arise and then attempt to practice them.

And who creates such opportunities? Not our friends, of course, but our enemies. They are the ones who give us the most trouble. So if we truly wish to learn, we should consider enemies to be our best teachers!

For a person who cherishes compassion and love, the practice of tolerance is essential, and for that, an enemy is indispensable. So we should feel grateful to our enemies, for it is they who can best help us develop a tranquil mind! Also, it is often the case in both personal and public life, that with a change in circumstances, enemies become friends.

So anger and hatred are always harmful, and unless we train our minds and work to reduce their negative force, they will continue to disturb us and disrupt our attempts to develop a calm mind. Anger and hatred are our real enemies. These are the forces we most need to confront and defeat, not the temporary "enemies" who appear intermittently throughout life.

Of course, it is natural and right that we all want friends. I often joke that if you really want to be selfish, you should be very altruistic! You should take good care of others, be concerned for their welfare, help them, serve them, make more friends, make more smiles. The result? When you yourself need help, you find plenty of helpers! If, on the other hand, you neglect the happiness of others, in the long term you will be the loser. And is friendship produced through quarrels and anger, jealousy and intense competitiveness? I do not think so. Only affection brings us genuine close friends.

In today's materialistic society, if you have money and power, you seem to have many friends.

But they are not friends of yours; they are the friends of your money and power. When you lose your wealth and influence, you will find it very difficult to track these people down.

The trouble is that when things in the world go well for us, we become confident that we can manage by ourselves and feel we do not need friends, but as our status and health decline, we quickly realize how wrong we were. That is the moment when we learn who is really helpful and who is completely useless. So to prepare for that moment, to make genuine friends who will help us when the need arises, we ourselves must cultivate altruism!

Though sometimes people laugh when I say it, I myself always want more friends. I love smiles. Because of this I have the problem of knowing how to make more friends and how to get more smiles, in particular, genuine smiles. For there are many kinds of smiles, such as sarcastic, artificial or diplomatic smiles. Many smiles produce no feeling of satisfaction, and sometimes they can even create suspicion or fear, can't they? But a genuine smile really gives us a feeling of freshness and is, I believe, unique to human beings. If these are the smiles we want, then we ourselves must create the reasons for them to appear.

Compassion and the world

In conclusion, I would like briefly to expand my

thoughts beyond the topic of this short piece and make a wider point: individual happiness can contribute in a profound and effective way to the overall improvement of our entire human community.

Because we all share an identical need for love, it is possible to feel that anybody we meet, in whatever circumstances, is a brother or sister. No matter how new the face or how different the dress and behavior, there is no significant division between us and other people. It is foolish to dwell on external differences, because our basic natures are the same.

Ultimately, humanity is one and this small planet is our only home. If we are to protect this home of ours, each of us needs to experience a vivid sense of universal altruism. It is only this feeling that can remove the self-centered motives that cause people to deceive and misuse one another. If you have a sincere and open heart, you naturally feel self-worth and confidence, and there is no need to be fearful of others.

I believe that at every level of society—familial, tribal, national and international— the key to a happier and more successful world is the growth of compassion. We do not need to become religious, nor do we need to believe in an ideology. All that is necessary is for each of us to develop our good human qualities.

I try to treat whoever I meet as an old friend. This gives me a genuine feeling of happiness. It is the practice of compassion.

The Global Community
and the Need for
Universal Responsibility

I believe that every individual has a responsibility to help guide our global family in the right direction. Good wishes alone are not enough; we have to assume responsibility. Large human movements spring from individual human initiatives. If you feel that you cannot have much of an effect, the next person may also become discouraged and a great opportunity will have been lost. On the other hand, each of us can inspire others simply by working to develop our own altruistic motivation.

The global community

As the twentieth century draws to a close, we find that the world has grown smaller and the world's people have become almost one community. Political and military alliances have created large multinational groups, industry and international trade have produced a global economy, and worldwide communications are eliminating ancient barriers of distance, language and race. We are also being drawn together by the grave problems we face: over-population, dwindling natural resources, and an environmental crisis that threatens our air, water, and trees, along with the vast number of beautiful life forms that are the very foundation of existence on this small planet we share.

I believe that to meet the challenge of our times, human beings will have to develop a greater sense of universal responsibility. Each of us must learn to work not just for his or her own self, family or nation, but for the benefit of all mankind. Universal responsibility is the real key to human survival. It is the best foundation for world peace, the equitable use of natural resources, and through concern for future generations, the proper care of the environment.

For some time, I have been thinking about how to increase our sense of mutual responsibility and the altruistic motive from which it derives. Briefly, I would like to offer my thoughts.

One human family

Whether we like it or not, we have all been born on this earth as part of one great human family. Rich or poor, educated or uneducated, belonging to one nation or another, to one religion or another, adhering to this ideology or that, ultimately each of us is just a human being like everyone else: we all desire happiness and do not want suffering. Furthermore, each of us has an equal right to pursue these goals.

Today's world requires that we accept the oneness of humanity. In the past, isolated communities could afford to think of one another as fundamentally separate and even existed in total isolation. Nowadays, however, events in one part of the world eventually affect the entire planet. Therefore we have to treat each major local problem as a global concern from the moment it begins. We can no longer invoke the national, racial or ideological barriers that separate us without destructive repercussion. In the context of our new interdependence, considering the interests of others is clearly the best form of self-interest.

I view this fact as a source of hope. The necessity for cooperation can only strengthen mankind, because it helps us recognize that the most secure foundation for the new world order is not simply broader political and economic alliances, but rather each individual's genuine practice of love and compassion. For a better, happier, more stable and civilized future, each of us must develop a sincere, warm-hearted feeling of brother- and sisterhood.

The medicine of altruism

In Tibet we say that many illnesses can be cured by the one medicine of love and compassion. These qualities are the ultimate source of human happiness, and our need for them lies at the very core of our being. Unfortunately, love and compassion have been omitted from too many spheres of social interaction for too long. Usually confined to family and home, their practice in public life is considered impractical, even naive. This is tragic. In my view, the practice of compassion is not just a symptom of unrealistic idealism but the most effective way to pursue the best interests of others as well as our own. The more we— as a nation, a group or as individuals— depend upon others, the more it is in our own best interests to ensure their well-being.

Practicing altruism is the real source of compromise and cooperation; merely recognizing our need for harmony is not enough. A mind committed to compassion is like an overflowing reservoir— a constant source of energy, determination and kindness. This mind is like a seed; when cultivated, it gives rise to many other good qualities, such as forgiveness, tolerance, inner strength and the confidence to overcome fear and insecurity. The compassionate mind is like an elixir; it is capable of transforming bad situations into beneficial ones. Therefore, we should not limit our expressions of love and compassion to our family and friends. Nor is compassion only the responsibility of clergy, health care and social workers. It is the necessary business of every part of the human community.

Whether a conflict lies in the field of politics, business or religion, an altruistic approach is frequently the sole means of resolving it. Sometimes the very concepts we use to mediate a dispute are themselves the cause of the problem. At such times, when a resolution seems impossible, both sides should recall the basic human nature that unites them. This will help break the impasse and, in the long run, make it easier for everyone to attain their goal. Although neither side may be fully satisfied, if both make concessions, at the very least, the danger of further conflict will be averted. We all know that this form of compromise is the most effective way of solving problems— why, then, do we not use it more often?

When I consider the lack of cooperation in human society, I can only conclude that it stems from ignorance of our interdependent nature. I am often moved by the example of small insects, such as bees. The laws of nature dictate that bees work together in order to survive. As a result, they possess an instinctive sense of social responsibility. They have no constitution, laws, police, religion or moral training, but because of their nature they labor faithfully together. Occasionally they may fight, but in general the whole colony survives on the basis of cooperation. Human beings, on the other hand, have constitutions, vast legal systems and police forces; we have religion, remarkable intelligence and a heart with a great capacity to love. But despite our many extraordinary qualities, in actual practice we lag behind those small insects; in some ways, I feel we are poorer than the bees.

For instance, millions of people live together in large cities all over the world, but despite this proximity, many are lonely. Some do not have even one human being with whom to share their deepest feelings, and live in a state of perpetual agitation. This is very sad. We are not solitary animals that associate only in order to mate. If we were, why would we build large cities and towns? But even though we are social animals compelled to live together, unfortunately, we lack a sense of responsibility towards our fellow humans. Does the fault lie in our social architecture— the basic structures of family and community that support our society? Is it in our external facilities— our machines, science and technology? I do not think so.

I believe that despite the rapid advances made by civilization in this century, the most immediate cause of our present dilemma is our undue emphasis on material development alone. We have become so engrossed in its pursuit that, without even knowing it, we have neglected to foster the most basic human needs of love, kindness, cooperation and caring. If we do not know someone or find another reason for not feeling connected with a particular individual or group, we simply ignore them. But the development of human society is based entirely on people helping each other. Once we have lost the essential humanity that is our foundation, what is the point of pursuing only material improvement?

To me, it is clear: a genuine sense of responsibility can result only if we develop compassion. Only a spontaneous feeling of empathy for others can really motivate us to act on their behalf. I have explained how to cultivate compassion elsewhere. For the remainder of this short piece, I would like to discuss how our present global situation can be improved by greater reliance on universal responsibility.

Universal responsibility

First, I should mention that I do not believe in creating movements or espousing ideologies. Nor do I like the practice of establishing an organization to promote a particular idea, which implies that one group of people alone is responsible for the attainment of that goal, while everybody else is exempt. In our present circumstances, none of us can afford to assume that somebody else will solve our problems; each of us must take his or her own share of universal responsibility. In this way, as the number of concerned, responsible individuals grows, tens, hundreds, thousands or even hundreds of thousands of such people will greatly improve the general atmosphere. Positive change does not come quickly and demands ongoing effort. If we become discouraged we may not attain even the simplest goals. With constant, determined application, we can accomplish even the most difficult objectives.

Adopting an attitude of universal responsibility is essentially a personal matter. The real test of compassion is not what we say in abstract discussions but how we conduct ourselves in daily life. Still, certain fundamental views are basic to the practice of altruism.

Though no system of government is perfect, democracy is that which is closest to humanity's essential nature. Hence those of us who enjoy it must continue to fight for all people's right to do so. Furthermore, democracy is the only stable foundation upon which a global political structure can be built. To work as one, we must respect the right of all peoples and nations to maintain their own distinctive character and values.

In particular, a tremendous effort will be required to bring compassion into the realm of international business. Economic inequality, especially that between developed and developing nations, remains the greatest source of suffering on this planet. Even though they will lose money in the short term, large multinational corporations must curtail their exploitation of poor nations. Tapping the few precious resources such countries possess simply to fuel consumerism in the developed world is disastrous; if it continues unchecked, eventually we shall all suffer. Strengthening weak, un-diversified economies is a far wiser policy for promoting both political and economic stability. As idealistic as it may sound, altruism, not just competition and the desire for wealth, should be a driving force in business.

We also need to renew our commitment to human values in the field of modern science. Though the main purpose of science is to learn more about reality, another of its goals is to improve the quality of life. Without altruistic motivation, scientists cannot distinguish between beneficial technologies and the merely expedient. The environmental damage surrounding us is the most obvious example of the result of this confusion, but proper motivation may be even more relevant in governing how we handle the extraordinary new array of biological techniques with which we can now manipulate the subtle structures of life itself. If we do not base our every action on an ethical foundation, we run the risk of inflicting terrible harm on the delicate matrix of life.

Nor are the religions of the world exempt from this responsibility. The purpose of religion is not to build beautiful churches or temples, but to cultivate positive human qualities such as tolerance, generosity and love. Every world religion, no matter what its philosophical view, is founded first and foremost on the precept that we must reduce our selfishness and serve others. Unfortunately, sometimes religion itself causes more quarrels than it solves. Practitioners of different faiths should realize that each religious tradition has immense intrinsic value and the means for providing mental and spiritual health. One religion, like a single type of food, cannot satisfy everybody. According to their varying mental dispositions, some people benefit from one kind of teaching, others from another. Each faith has the ability to produce fine, warmhearted people and all religions have succeeded in doing so, despite their espousal of often contradictory philosophies. Thus there is no reason to engage in divisive religious bigotry and intolerance and every reason to cherish and respect all forms of spiritual practice.

Certainly, the most important field in which to sow the seeds of greater altruism is international relations. In the past few years the world has changed dramatically. I think we would all agree that the end of the Cold War and the collapse of communism in Eastern Europe and the former Soviet Union have ushered in a new historical era. As we move through the 1990s it would seem that human experience in the twentieth century has come full circle.

This has been the most painful period in human history, a time when, because of the vast increase in the destructive power of weapons, more people have suffered from and died by violence than ever before. Furthermore, we have also witnessed an almost terminal competition between the fundamental ideologies that have always torn the human community: force and raw power on the one hand, and freedom, pluralism, individual rights and democracy on the other. I believe that the results of this great competition are now clear. Though the good human spirit of peace, freedom and democracy still faces many form of tyranny and evil, it is nevertheless an unmistakable fact that the vast majority of people everywhere want it to triumph. Thus the tragedies of our time have not been entirely without benefit, and in many cases have been the very means by which the human mind has been opened. The collapse of communism demonstrate this.

Although communism espoused many noble ideals, including altruism, the attempt by its governing elites to dictate their views has proved disastrous. These governments went to tremendous lengths to control the entire flow of information through their societies and to structure their education systems so that their citizens would work for the common good. Although rigid organization may have been necessary in the beginning to destroy previously oppressive regimes, once that goal was fulfilled, the organization had very little to contribute towards building a useful human community. Communism failed utterly because it relied on force to promote its beliefs. Ultimately, human nature was unable to sustain the suffering it produced.

Brute force, no matter how strongly applied, can never subdue the basic human desire for freedom. The hundreds of thousands of people who marched in the cities of Eastern Europe proved this. They simply expressed the human need for freedom and democracy. It was very moving. Their demands had nothing whatsoever to do with some new ideology; these people simply spoke from their hearts, sharing their desire for freedom, demonstrating that it stems from the core of human nature. Freedom, in fact, is the very source of creativity for both individuals and society. It is not enough, as communist systems have assumed, merely to provide people with food, shelter and clothing. If we have all these things but lack the precious air of liberty to sustain our deeper nature, we are only half human; we are like animals who are content just to satisfy their physical needs.

I feel that the peaceful revolutions in the former Soviet Union and Eastern Europe have taught us many great lessons. One is the value of truth. People do not like to be bullied, cheated or lied to by either an individual or a system. Such acts are contrary to the essential human spirit. Therefore, even though those who practice deception and use force may achieve considerable short-term success, eventually they will be overthrown.

On the other hand, everyone appreciates truth, and respect for it is really in our blood. Truth is the best guarantor and the real foundation of freedom and democracy. It does not matter whether you are weak or strong or whether your cause has many or few adherents, truth will still prevail. The fact that the successful freedom movements of 1989 and after have been based on the true expression of people's most basic feelings is a valuable reminder that truth itself is still seriously lacking in much of our political life. Especially in the conduct of international relations we pay very little respect to truth. Inevitably, weaker nations are manipulated and oppressed by stronger ones, just as the weaker sections of most societies suffer at the hands of the more affluent and powerful. Though in the past, the simple expression of truth has usually been dismissed as unrealistic, these last few years have proved that it is an immense force in the human mind and as a result, in the shaping of history.

A second great lesson from Eastern Europe has been that of peaceful change. In the past, enslaved peoples often resorted to violence in their struggle to be free. Now, following in the footsteps of Mahatma Gandhi and Martin Luther King, Jr., these peaceful revolutions offer future generations a wonderful example of successful, nonviolent change. When in the future major changes in society again become necessary, our descendants will be able to look back on the present time as a paradigm of peaceful struggle, a real success story of unprecedented scale, involving more than a dozen nations and hundreds of millions of people. Moreover, recent events have shown that the desire for both peace and freedom lies at the most fundamental level of human nature and that violence is its complete antithesis.

Before considering what kind of global order would serve us best in the post-cold War period, I think it is vital to address the question of violence, whose elimination at every level is the necessary foundation for world peace and the ultimate goal of any international order.

Nonviolence and international order

Every day the media reports incidents of terrorism, crime and aggression. I have never been to a country where tragic stories of death and bloodshed did not fill the newspapers and airwaves. Such reporting has become almost an addiction for journalists and their audiences alike. But the overwhelming majority of the human race does not behave destructively; very few of the five billion people on this planet actually commit acts of violence. Most of us prefer to be as peaceful as possible.

Basically, we all cherish tranquility, even those of us given to violence. For instance, when spring comes, the days grow longer, there is more sunshine, the grass and trees come alive and everything is very fresh. People feel happy. In autumn, one leaf falls, then another, then all the beautiful flowers die until we are surrounded by bare, naked plants. We do not feel so joyful. Why is this? Because deep down, we desire constructive, fruitful growth and dislike things collapsing, dying or being destroyed. Every destructive action goes against our basic nature; building, being constructive, is the human way.

I am sure everybody agrees that we need to overcome violence, but if we are to eliminate it completely, we should first analyze whether or not it has any value.

If we address this question from a strictly practical perspective, we find that on certain occasions violence indeed appears useful. One can solve a problem quickly with force. At the same time, however, such success is often at the expense of the rights and welfare of others. As a result, even though one problem has been solved, the seed of another has been planted.

On the other hand, if one's cause is supported by sound reasoning, there is no point in using violence. It is those who have no motive other than selfish desire and who cannot achieve their goal through logical reasoning who rely on force. Even when family and friends disagree, those with valid reasons can cite them one after the other and argue their case point by point, whereas those with little rational support soon fall prey to anger. Thus anger is not a sign of strength but one of weakness.

Ultimately, it is important to examine one's own motivation and that of one's opponent. There are many kinds of violence and nonviolence, but one cannot distinguish them from external factors alone. If one's motivation is negative, the action it produces is, in the deepest sense, violent, even though it may appear to be smooth and gentle. Conversely, if one's motivation is sincere and positive but the circumstances require harsh behavior, essentially one is practicing nonviolence. No matter what the case may be, I feel that a compassionate concern for the benefit of others— not simply for oneself— is the sole justification for the use of force.

The genuine practice of nonviolence is still somewhat experimental on our planet, but its pursuit, based on love and understanding, is sacred. If this experiment succeeds, it can open the way to a far more peaceful world in the next century.

I have heard the occasional Westerner maintain that long-term Gandhian struggles employing nonviolent passive resistance do not suit everybody and that such courses of action are more natural in the East. Because Westerners are active, they tend to seek immediate results in all situations, even at the cost of their lives. This approach, I believe, is not always beneficial. But surely the practice of non-violence suits us all. It simply calls for determination. Even though the freedom movements of Eastern Europe reached their goals quickly, nonviolent protest by its very nature usually require patience.

In this regard, I pray that despite the brutality

of their suppression and the difficulty of the struggle they face, those involved in China's democracy movement will always remain peaceful. I am confident they will. Although the majority of the young Chinese students involved were born and raised under an especially harsh form of communism, during the spring of 1989 they spontaneously practiced Mahatma Gandhi's strategy of passive resistance. This is remarkable and clearly shows that ultimately all human beings want to pursue the path of peace, no matter how much they have been indoctrinated.

The reality of war

Of course, war and the large military establishments are the greatest sources of violence in the world. Whether their purpose is defensive or offensive, these vast powerful organizations exist solely to kill human beings. We should think carefully about the reality of war. Most of us have been conditioned to regard military combat as exciting and glamorous— an opportunity for men to prove their competence and courage. Since armies are legal, we feel that war is acceptable; in general, nobody feels that war is criminal or that accepting it is a criminal attitude. In fact, we have been brainwashed. War is neither glamorous nor attractive. It is monstrous. Its very nature is one of tragedy and suffering.

War is like a fire in the human community, one whose fuel is living beings. I find this analogy especially appropriate and useful. Modern warfare is waged primarily with different forms of fire, but we are so conditioned to see it as thrilling that we talk about this or that marvelous weapon as a remarkable piece of technology without remembering that, if it is actually used, it will burn living people. War also strongly resembles a fire in the way it spreads. If one area gets weak, the commanding officer sends reinforcements. This is like throwing live people onto a fire. But because we have been brainwashed to think this way, we do not consider the suffering of individual soldiers. No soldier wants to be wounded or die; none of his loved ones wants any harm to come to him. If one soldier is killed, or maimed for life, at least another five or ten people— his relatives and friends— suffer as well. We should all be horrified by the extent of this tragedy, but we are too confused.

Frankly, as a child, I too was attracted to the military. Their uniforms looked so smart and beautiful. But that is exactly how the seduction begins. Children start playing games that will one day lead them into trouble. There are plenty of exciting games to play and costumes to wear other than those based on the killing of human beings. Again, if we as adults were not so fascinated by war, we would clearly see that to allow our children to become habituated to war games is extremely unfortunate. Some former soldiers have told me that when they shot their first person they felt uncomfortable but as they continued to kill it began to feel quite normal. In time, we can get used to anything.

It is not only during times of war that military establishments are destructive. By their very design, they are the single greatest violators of human rights, and it is the soldiers themselves who suffer most consistently from their abuse. After the officers in charge have given beautiful explanations about the importance of the army, its discipline and the need to conquer the enemy, the rights of the great mass of soldiers are almost entirely taken away. They are then compelled to forfeit their individual will, and, in the end, to sacrifice their lives. Moreover, once an army has become a powerful force, there is every risk that it will destroy the happiness of its own country.

There are people with destructive intentions in every society, and the temptation to gain command over an organization capable of fulfilling their desires can become overwhelming. But no matter how malevolent or evil are the many murderous dictators who currently oppress their nations and cause international problems, it is obvious that they cannot harm others or destroy countless human lives if they don't have a military organization accepted and condoned by society. As long as there are powerful armies there will always be the danger of dictatorship. If we really believe dictatorship to be a despicable and destructive form of government, then we must recognize that the existence of a powerful military establishment is one of its main causes.

Militarism is also very expensive. Pursuing peace through military strength places a tremendously wasteful burden on society. Governments spend vast sums on increasingly intricate weapons when, in fact, nobody really wants to use them. Not only money but also valuable energy and human intelligence are squandered, while all that increases is fear.

I want to make it clear, however, that although I am deeply opposed to war, I am not advocating appeasement. It is often necessary to take a strong stand to counter unjust aggression. For instance, it is plain to all of us that the Second World War was entirely justified. It "saved civilization" from the tyranny of Nazi Germany, as Winston Churchill so aptly put it. In my view, the Korean War was also just, since it gave South Korea the chance of gradually developing democracy. But we can only judge whether or not a conflict was vindicated on moral grounds with hindsight. For example, we can now see that during the Cold War, the principle of nuclear deterrence had a certain value. Nevertheless, it is very difficult to assess all such matters with any degree of accuracy. War is violence and violence is unpredictable. Therefore, it is far better to avoid it if possible, and never to presume that we know beforehand whether the outcome of a particular war will be beneficial or not.

For instance, in the case of the Cold War, though deterrence may have helped promote stability, it did not create genuine peace. The last forty years in Europe have seen merely the absence of war, which has not been real peace but a facsimile founded on fear. At best, building arms to maintain peace serves only as a temporary measure. As long as adversaries do not trust each other, any number of factors can upset the balance of power. Lasting peace can be secured only on the basis of genuine trust.

Disarmament for world peace

Throughout history, mankind has pursued peace one way or another. Is it too optimistic to imagine that world peace may finally be within our grasp? I do not believe that there has been an increase in the amount of people's hatred, only in their ability to manifest it is vastly destructive weapons. On the other hand, bearing witness to the tragic evidence of the mass slaughter caused by such weapons in our century has given us the opportunity to control war. To do so, it is clear we must disarm.

Disarmament can occur only within the context of new political and economic relationships. Before we consider this issue in detail, it is worth imagining the kind of peace process from which we would benefit most. This is fairly self-evident. First we should work on eliminating nuclear weapons, next, biological and chemical ones, then offensive arms, and, finally, defensive ones. At the same time, to safeguard the peace, we should start developing in one or more global regions an international police force made up of an equal number of members from each nation under a collective command. Eventually this force would cover the whole world.

Because the dual process of disarmament and development of a joint force would be both multilateral and democratic, the right of the majority to criticize or even intervene in the event of one nation violating the basic rules would be ensured. Moreover, with all large armies eliminated and all conflicts such as border disputes subject to the control of the joint international force, large and small nations would be truly equal. Such reforms would result in a stable international environment.

Of course, the immense financial dividend reaped from the cessation of arms production would also provide a fantastic windfall for global development. Today, the nations of the world spend trillions of dollars annually on upkeep of the military. Can you imagine how many hospital beds, schools and homes this money could fund? In addition, as I mentioned above, the awesome proportion of scarce resources squandered on military development not only prevents the elimination of poverty, illiteracy and disease, but also requires the sacrifice of precious human intelligence. Our scientists are extremely bright. Why should their brilliance be wasted on such dreadful endeavors when it could be used for positive global development?

The great deserts of the world such as the

Sahara and the Gobi could be cultivated to increase food production and ease overcrowding. Many countries now face years of severe drought. New, less expensive methods of desalinization could be developed to render sea water suitable for human consumption and other uses. There are many pressing issues in the fields of energy and health to which our scientists could more usefully address themselves. Since the world economy would grow more rapidly as a result of their efforts, they could even be paid more!

Our planet is blessed with vast natural treasures. If we use them properly, beginning with the elimination of militarism and war, truly, every human being will be able to live a wealthy, well-cared-for life.

Naturally, global peace cannot occur all at once. Since conditions around the world are so varied, its spread will have to be incremental. But there is no reason why it cannot begin in one region and then spread gradually from one continent to another.

I would like to propose that regional communities like the European Community be established as an integral part of the more peaceful world we are trying to create. Looking at the post-Cold War environment objectively, such communities are plainly the most natural and desirable components of a new world order. As we can see, the almost gravitational pull of our growing interdependence necessitates new, more cooperative structures. The European Community is pioneering the way in this endeavor, negotiating the delicate balance between economic, military and political collectivity on the one hand and the sovereign rights of member states on the other. I am greatly inspired by this work. I also believe that the new Commonwealth of Independent States is grappling with similar issues and that the seeds of such a community are already present in the minds of many of its constituent republics. In this context, I would briefly like to talk about the future of both my own country, Tibet, and China.

Like the former Soviet Union, Communist China is a multinational state, artificially constructed under the impetus of an expansionist ideology and up to now administered by force in colonial fashion. A peaceful, prosperous and above all politically stable future for China lies in its successfully fulfilling not only its own people's wishes for a more open, democratic system, but also those of its eighty million so-called "national minorities", who want to regain their freedom. For real happiness to return to the heart of Asia— home to one-fifth of the human race—a pluralistic, democratic, mutually cooperative community of sovereign states must replace what is currently called the People's Republic of China.

Of course, such a community need not be limited to those presently under Chinese Communist domination, such as Tibetans, Mongols and Uighurs. The people of Hong Kong, those seeking an independent Taiwan, and even those suffering under other communist governments in

North Korea, Vietnam, Laos and Cambodia might also be interested in building an Asian Community. However, it is especially urgent that those ruled by the Chinese Communists consider doing so. Properly pursued, it could help save China from violent dissolution, regionalism and a return to the chaotic turmoil that has so afflicted this great nation throughout the twentieth century. Currently China's political life is so polarized that there is every reason to fear an early recurrence of bloodshed and tragedy. Each of us— every member of the world community— has a moral responsibility to help avert the immense suffering that civil strife would bring to China's vast population.

I believe that the very process of dialogue, moderation and compromise involved in building a community of Asian states would itself give real hope of peaceful evolution to a new order in China. From the very start, the member states of such a community might agree to decide its defense and international relations policies together. There would be many opportunities for cooperation. The critical point is that we find a peaceful, nonviolent way for the forces of freedom, democracy and moderation to emerge successfully from the current atmosphere of unjust repression.

Zones of peace

I see Tibet's role in such an Asian Community as what I have previously called a "Zone of Peace": a neutral, demilitarized sanctuary where weapons are forbidden and the people live in harmony with nature. This is not merely a dream— it is precisely the way Tibetans tried to live for over a thousand years before our country was invaded. As everybody knows, in Tibet all forms of wildlife were strictly protected in accordance with Buddhist principles. Also, for at least the last three hundred years, we had no proper army. Tibet gave up the waging of war as an instrument of national policy in the sixth and seventh centuries, after the reign of our three great religious kings.

Returning to the relationship between developing regional communities and the task of disarmament, I would like to suggest that the "heart" of each community could be one or more nations that have decided to become zones of peace, areas from which military forces are prohibited. This, again, is not just a dream. Four decades ago, in December 1948, Costa Rica disbanded its army. Recently, 37 per cent of Swiss population voted to disband their military. The new government of Czechoslovakia has decided to stop the manufacture and export of all weapons. If its people so choose, a nation can take radical steps to change its very nature.

Zones of peace within regional communities

would serve as oasis of stability. While paying
their fair share of the costs of any collective force
created by the community as a whole, these zones
of peace would be the forerunners and beacons
of an entirely peaceful world and would be exempt
from engaging in any conflict. If regional
communities do develop in Asia, South America
and Africa and disarmament progresses so that an
international force from all regions is created,
these zones of peace will be able to expand,
spreading tranquility as they grow.

We do not need to think that we are planning
for the far distant future when we consider this or
any other proposal for a new, more politically,
economically and militarily cooperative world.
For instance, the newly invigorated forty-eight
member conference on Security and Cooperation
in Europe has already laid the foundation for an
alliance between not only the nations of Eastern
and Western Europe— but also between the
nations of the Commonwealth of Independent
States and the United States. These remarkable
events have virtually eliminated the danger of a
major war between these two superpowers.

I have not included the United Nations in this
discussion of the present era because both its
critical role in helping create a better world and
its great potential for doing so are so well known.
By definition, the United Nations must be in the
very middle of whatever major changes occur.
However, it may need to amend its structure for
the future. I have always had the greatest hopes

for the United Nations, and with no criticism intended, I would like simply to point out that the post-World War II climate under which its charter was conceived has changed. With that change has come the opportunity to further democratize the UN, especially the somewhat exclusive Security Council with its five permanent members, which should be made more representative.

In conclusion

I would like to conclude by stating that, in general, I feel optimistic about the future. Some recent trends portend our great potential for a better world. As late as the fifties and sixties, people believed that war was an inevitable condition of mankind. The Cold War, in particular, reinforced the notion that opposing political systems could only clash, not compete or even collaborate. Few now hold this view. Today, people all over the planet are genuinely concerned about world peace. They are far less interested in propounding ideology and far more committed to coexistence. These are very positive developments.

Also, for thousands of years people believed that only an authoritarian organization employing rigid disciplinary methods could govern human society. However, people have an innate desire for freedom and democracy, and these two forces have been in conflict. Today, it is clear which has won. The emergence of nonviolent "people's power" movements have shown indisputably that the human race can neither tolerate nor function properly under the rule of tyranny. This recognition represents remarkable progress.

Another hopeful development is the growing compatibility between science and religion. Throughout the nineteenth century and for much of our own, people have been profoundly confused by the conflict between these apparently contradictory world views. Today, physics, biology and psychology have reached such sophisticated levels that many researchers are starting to ask the most profound questions about the ultimate nature of the universe and life, the same questions that are of prime interest to religions. Thus there is real potential for a more unified view. In particular, it seems that a new concept of mind and matter is emerging. The East has been more concerned with understanding the mind, the West with understanding matter. Now that the two have met, these spiritual and material views of life may become more harmonized.

The rapid changes in our attitude towards the earth are also a source of hope. As recently as ten or fifteen years ago, we thoughtlessly consumed its resources, as if there was no end to them. Now, not only individuals but governments as well are seeking a new ecological order. I often joke that the moon and stars look beautiful, but if any of us tried to live on them, we would be miserable. This blue planet of ours is the most delightful habitat we know. Its life is our life; its future, our future. And though I do not believe that the Earth itself is a sentient being, it does indeed act as our mother, and, like children, we are dependent upon her. Now mother nature is telling us to cooperate. In the face of such global problems as the greenhouse effect and the deterioration of the ozone layer, individual organizations and single nations are helpless. Unless we all work together, no solution will be found. Our mother is teaching us a lesson in universal responsibility.

I think we can say that, because of the lessons we have begun to learn, the next century will be friendlier, more harmonious, and less harmful. Compassion, the seed of peace, will be able to flourish. I am very hopeful. At the same time, I believe that every individual has a responsibility to help guide our global family in the right direction. Good wishes alone are not enough; we have to assume responsibility. Large human movements spring from individual human initiatives. If you feel that you cannot have much of an effect, the next person may also become discouraged and a great opportunity will have been lost. On the other hand, each of us can inspire others simply by working to develop our own altruistic motivation.

I am sure that many honest, sincere people all over the world already hold that views that I have mentioned here. Unfortunately, nobody listens to them. Although my voice may go unheeded as well, I thought that I should try to speak on their behalf. Of course, some people may feel that it is very presumptuous for the Dalai Lama to write in this way. But, since I received the Nobel Peace Prize, I feel I have a responsibility to do so. If I just took the Nobel money and spent it however I liked, it would look as if the only reason I had spoken all those nice words in the past was to get this prize! However, now that I have received it, I must repay the honor by continuing to advocate the views that I have always expressed.

I, for one, truly believe that individuals can make difference in society. Since periods of great change such as the present one come so rarely in human history, it is up to each of us to make the best use of our time to help create a happier world.

●●●●●●●●●●●●●●●●●●●●

May all sentient beings,
oneself and others,
find constant happiness through
love and compassion
associated with wisdom.